101 COOL CANADIAN JOKES

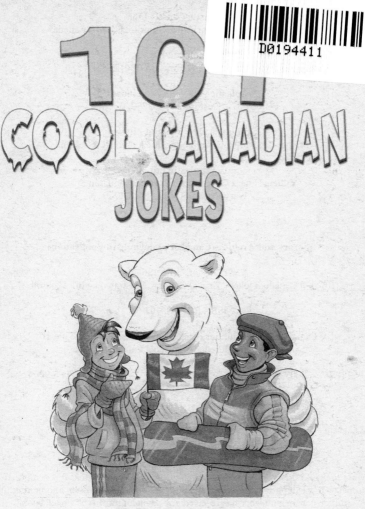

Erin O'Connor

Illustrated by
Bill Dickson

Scholastic Canada Ltd.
Toronto New York London Auckland Sydney
Mexico City New Delhi Hong Kong Buenos Aires

Scholastic Canada Ltd.
175 Hillmount Road, Markham, Ontario L6C 1Z7, Canada

Scholastic Inc.
555 Broadway, New York, NY 10012, USA

Scholastic Australia Pty Limited
PO Box 579, Gosford, NSW 2250, Australia

Scholastic New Zealand Limited
Private Bag 94407, Greenmount, Auckland, New Zealand

Scholastic Ltd.
Villiers House, Clarendon Avenue, Leamington Spa,
Warwickshire CV32 5PR, UK

Library and Archives Canada Cataloguing in Publication

O'Connor, Erin, 1968 -
101 cool Canadian jokes / Erin O'Connor ; illustrated by Bill Dickson.

ISBN 0-439-95205-0

1. Canadian wit and humor (English) I. Dickson, Bill II. Title. III.
Title: One hundred and one cool Canadian jokes.

PS8375.O26 2005   jC818'.602   C2005-900424-X

Text copyright © 2005 by Erin O'Connor.
Illustrations copyright © 2005 by Scholastic Canada Ltd.
All rights reserved.

If you purchased this book without a cover, you should be aware that this book is stolen
property. It was reported as "unsold and destroyed" to the publisher, and neither the
author nor the publisher has received any payment for this "stripped book."

No part of this publication may be reproduced or stored in a retrieval system,
or transmitted in any form or by any means, electronic, mechanical, recording,
or otherwise, without written permission of the publisher, Scholastic Canada Ltd.,
175 Hillmount Road, Markham, Ontario L6C 1Z7, Canada.
In the case of photocopying or other reprographic copying, a licence must be obtained
from Access Copyright (Canadian Copyright Licensing Agency),
1 Yonge Street, Suite 1900,
Toronto, Ontario M5E 1E5 (1-800-893-5777).

6 5 4 3 2 1   Printed in Canada   05 06 07 08 09

Wild Canada!

What should you do when you're surrounded by polar bears, cougars and killer whales?

Hope you're at the zoo!

What did the maple tree say to the woodpecker?

Leaf me alone!

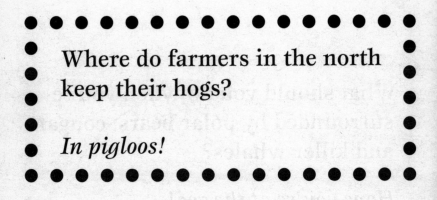

Where do farmers in the north keep their hogs?

In pigloos!

Where do husky dogs live?

In the Barktic!

What did the doctor say to the new mosquito mother?

There's a sucker born every minute!

Why did the otter cross the road?

To get to the other slide.

What airline do grizzlies fly?

Bear Canada.

What is the lake monster's favourite toy?

An Ogopogo stick.

What are the scariest animals?

CariBOOs!

How does Bigfoot tell time?

With a Sasquatch!

What do you get when you cross
a lobster with a supermodel?

A snappy dresser!

What do you get when you
cross a polar bear and a cougar?

*I don't know, but you'd better
run quick*

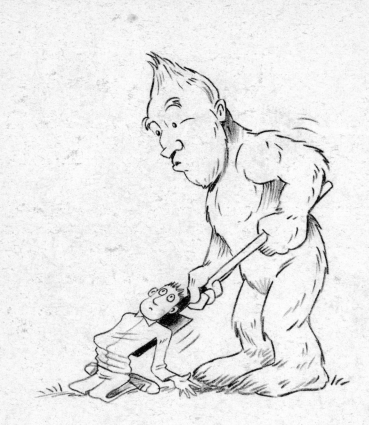

What would you be if 100 Bigfoots
fell on your head?

Sasquashed!

What kind of bug repellant does
a light bulb wear?

OFF!

What do you get when you cross
a pig with a killer whale?

A porca.

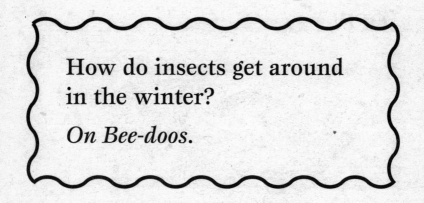

How do insects get around
in the winter?

On Bee-doos.

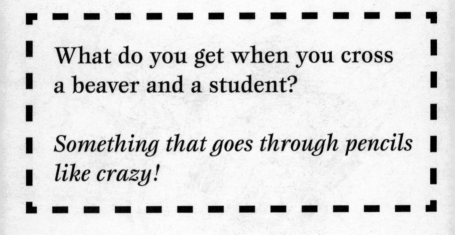

What do you get when you cross a beaver and a student?

Something that goes through pencils like crazy!

What did the Canada goose say to
the mallard?

You quack me up!

What do you get when you cross
a walrus with a shopaholic?

A mallrus!

What did the elk say to the caribou
when it fell through the ice?

Oh deer!

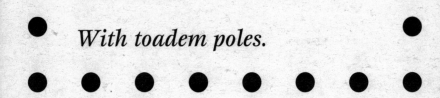

How do frogs honour their ancestors?

With toadem poles.

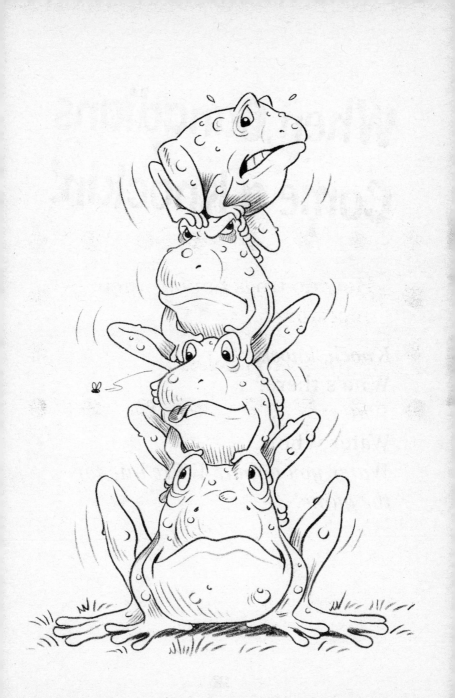

When Canadians Come a-Knockin'

Knock, knock.
Who's there?
Water.
Water who?
Water you doing? We're late for the game!

Knock, knock.
Who's there?
Icy.
Icy who?
Icy you're not expecting me!

Knock, knock.
Who's there?
Tuque.
Tuque who?
Tuque you by surprise, didn't I?

Knock, knock.
Who's there?
Dishes.
Dishes who?
Dishes the RCMP – open up!

Knock, knock.
Who's there?
Snow.
Snow who?
*Snow fun standing out here
in the cold!*

Knock, knock.
Who's there?
Yukon.
Yukon who?
Yukon let me in now!

Knock, knock.
Who's there?
Inukshuk.
Inukshuk who?
Gesundheit!

Knock, knock.
Who's there?
Wheat.
Wheat who?
*Wheat a minute — I've got
the wrong house!*

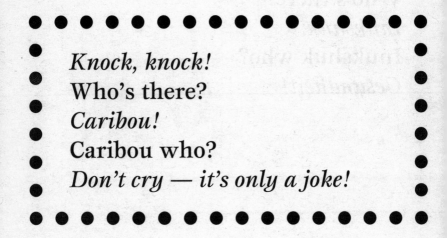

Knock, knock!
Who's there?
Caribou!
Caribou who?
Don't cry — it's only a joke!

Jokes for Jocks

What sport do bare feet like to play?

Ice sockey.

What sport do cats like to play?

Mice hockey.

What did the sporty chicken do?

He lacrossed the road.

Why did the paddle get a
cell phone?

It loved kayaking all the time.

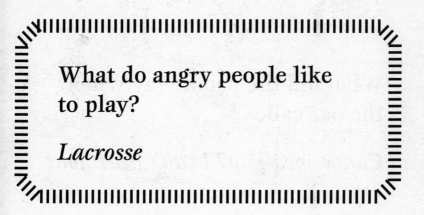

What do angry people like to play?

Lacrosse

What sport do circles like to play?

Ringette.

What did the paddle say when the oar called?

Canoe speak up? I can't hear you!

What do pigs clean the ice with?

A Hamboni.

What do you get when you cross
a great hockey player and
a plumber?

Drain Gretzky!

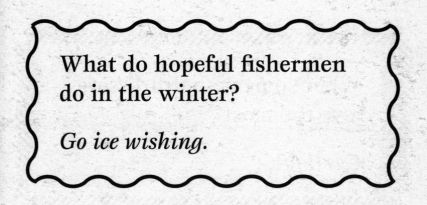

What do hopeful fishermen
do in the winter?

Go ice wishing.

What sport do hairdressers
love the most?

Curling!

What kind of rodents play hockey?

Rink rats!

What lives in water and plays hockey?

A skate fish.

What do squares like to play?

Ice blockey.

THOSE CRAZY CANUCKS

Why didn't anyone ask
the maple tree to the dance?

Because it wasn't poplar.

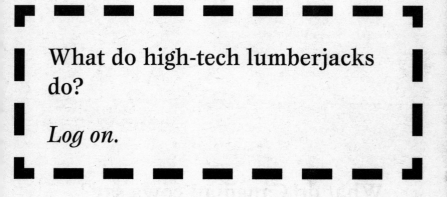

What do high-tech lumberjacks do?

Log on.

What do Canadian horses say?

N-eh?

What do Canadian cows say?

Moo, silly!

How does a Timbit get around in winter?

On doughshoes.

Why are Canadian students so smart?

They get a lot of ehs.

What do snowmen play with?

Teddy brrrrrs.

What do negative Canadians drive?

Ski-don'ts!

Where do arctic hamburgers
come from?

The bundra.

What kind of loot do Canadian pirates stash away?

Doubloonies.

What did Homer Simpson sing at the beginning of the hockey game?

D'oh Canada.

Where did the clumsy voyageur go?

On a canoe trip.

What do you call police officers just standing around?

The Royal Canadian Dismounted Police.

Where do happy campers sleep?

In teehees.

What did the patriotic snail sing?

Slow Canada.

How does a Mountie stay in the saddle?

With maple stirrups.

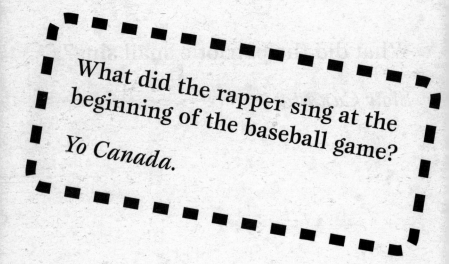

What did the rapper sing at the beginning of the baseball game?

Yo Canada.

What is the logger's favourite
nursery rhyme?

Lumberjack and Jill.

FROM SEA TO SILLY SEA

Where does the tallest man
in the world get clean?

The CN Shower.

What is the most amusing body of water in Canada?

The Bay of Fundy.

What's huge, green and found
in Sudbury, Ontario?

The Big Pickle!

What is bread made with
in Nunavut?

Iqaluwheat.

What mountains like to fight?

The Rocky Mountains!

There were 12 pieces of pie, but
13 provinces and territories —
who didn't get a piece?

Nunavut.

Where is the scariest place
in Canada?

The Yukon Terrortory.

What's the most annoying province?

Pinch Edward Island.

Where does the river always trip?

Niagara Falls!

Why did the envelope go to Calgary?

For the Stamp*ede.*

Which province is frightening?

Onscareio!

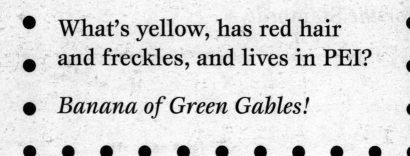

What's yellow, has red hair
and freckles, and lives in PEI?

Banana of Green Gables!

What caped crusader helps those in need across the Prairies?

Flatman!

Why is the Bay of Fundy so clean?

Because of the Tide.

Oh, You Canucklehead!

What do you call a foolish Canadian?

A Canucklehead!

Canucklehead: *Doctor, I feel like a jelly doughnut!*
Doctor: *What's gotten into you?*
Canucklehead: *Flour, sugar and raspberry filling.*

Canucklehead: *Doctor, my eye hurts every time I drink hot chocolate!*

Doctor: *Then take the spoon out of the cup first!*

Canucklehead: *Doctor, people are saying I'm crazy because I love doughnuts.*

Doctor: *That's nonsense. Lots of people love doughnuts.*

Canucklehead: *What a relief! Do you want to come to the wedding?*

Teacher: *Why is there a maple leaf on our flag?*

Canucklehead: *Because the whole tree wouldn't fit!*

Canucklehead: *Doctor, I swallowed a dollar!*
Doctor: *How do you feel?*
Canucklehead: *Loonie!*

Why did the Canucklehead bury his wallet in the snow?

He wanted cold, hard cash.

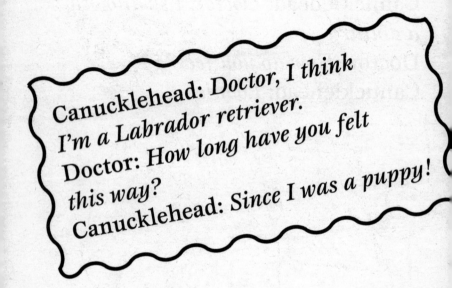

Canucklehead: Doctor, I think I'm a Labrador retriever.

Doctor: How long have you felt this way?

Canucklehead: Since I was a puppy!

Canucklehead: *Doctor, I feel awful. What's wrong with me?*
Doctor: *You've got doughnuts up your nose, poutine in your ears and maple syrup on your head. I don't think you're eating right.*

Canucklehead: *Doctor, I swallowed a whole doughnut.*
Doctor: *Are you choking?*
Canucklehead: *No, I'm telling the truth!*

Teacher: *Why are you wearing flippers to school?*
Canucklehead: *To keep grizzly bears away.*
Teacher: *But there aren't any grizzly bears around here.*
Canucklehead: *See — it works!*

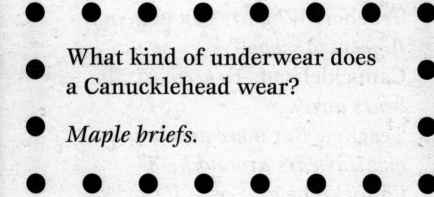

What kind of underwear does
a Canucklehead wear?

Maple briefs.

Why did the Canucklehead move up north to Tuktoyuktuk?

Because he wanted to be cool!

Why did the Canucklehead cross the road?

To prove he wasn't chicken.

Why did the Canucklehead stop
ice fishing?

The Zamboni was coming.

How do you keep a Canucklehead
in suspense?

I'll tell you tomorrow!

What happened to the
Canucklehead who thought he was
a Canada Goose?

He flew south for the winter!

Capital Humour

How do you make the prime minister fly?

Put him on a plane.

Where do pickles have their government buildings?

On Parliament Dill!

What do you get when you cross
the prime minister with a battery?

Someone who's really in charge!

What do you get when you cross
the prime minister with an owl?

Someone who gives a hoot!

Where do cyborg politicians
work?

In Robottawa!

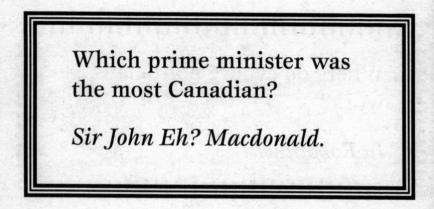

Which prime minister was the most Canadian?

Sir John Eh? Macdonald.

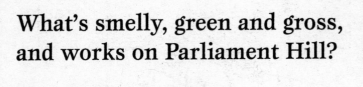

What's smelly, green and gross, and works on Parliament Hill?

The slime minister!

Top 10 Canadian Bestsellers:

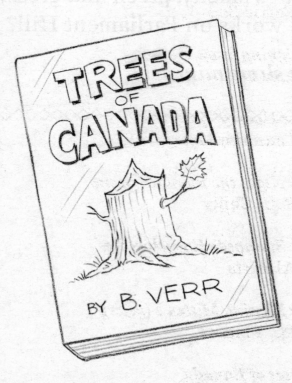

1. *Beavers: Friend or Foe?*
   by May Poll

2. *Canada: The Greatest Country in the World*
   by Ken Nuck

3. *The Wonderful World of Doughnuts*
   by I.M. Dieting

4. *Everything You Need to Know about
   Moss and Lichen*
   by Carrie Boo

5. *Designing Snow Houses*
   by Iggy Lou

6. *Once Upon a Waterway*
   by Laurence Seaway

7. *The Night the Furnace Broke*
   by R.U. Chilly

8. *The Stampede Encyclopedia*
   by Al Berta

9. *The Missing Mitten Mystery*
   by I.C. Fingers

10. *Trees of Canada*
    by B. Verr